□ THE NEW EDEN □

Sioux Buck Ghost Horse has written: *Humankind seeks Utopia, but strives for it through destruction of the Balance of the Earth. When the spiritual level of humankind reaches the level of balance held by nature then we will have the balance needed to regain Utopia which we once called Eden and Earth People call the Earth Mother.*

Creation Magazine 11:3 1987

Susan
Seddon
Boulet
1989

The New Eden

For People, Animals & Nature

By DR. MICHAEL W. FOX
With Illustrations by
SUSAN SEDDON BOULET

LOTUS PRESS

SANTA FE, NEW MEXICO

CONSULTING EDITOR: Alma S. King
BOOK DESIGN: Mina Yamashita Graphic Design/Sunstone Press

Susan Seddon Boulet's art appears courtesy of Pomegranate Calendars & Books, Petaluma, CA.

Library of Congress Cataloging-in-Publication Data

Fox, Michael W., 1937–
The New Eden: for people, animals & nature/by Michael W. Fox.
p. cm.
ISBN 0-941524-46-9: $8.95
1. Human ecology—Moral and ethical aspects. 2. Philosophy of nature. 3. Nature—Religious aspects. I. Title.
GF80.F65 1989
179'.1—dc20 89-12998
CIP

Published in 1989 by Lotus Press / P.O. Box 6265 /
Santa Fe, New Mexico 87502-6265

For Deanna

□ INTRODUCTION □

History informs that all civilizations in times of crisis have elaborated various mythologies to sustain them through the processes of disintegration, transformation and renewal. Today myth is commonly regarded as that which is false, non-rational, and illusory. Yet mythic visions were once part of the *ethos* and *eidos* of those civilizations that knew only too well that "where there is no vision the people shall perish."

What vision do we have today, in a world where nations are on the brink of thermonuclear conflagration and where nature is desacralized and degraded into an industrialized and polluted wasteland? The late U-Thant, Secretary of the United Nations, said that "Either we develop the first global civilization, provide for its conscious, direct growth, or we shall perish... If not with a 'big bang' of nuclear holocaust then with the whimper of a species which ran out of air, water, resources and food."

The vision of a technological utopia, of material affluence and absolute control over the environment and natural creation is a myth we must abandon if we cannot democratize it with respect to the whole of creation, even though our power over the atoms of matter and the genes of life seem to affirm that it is still within our reach. Lao Tzu advised some 3,000 years ago, "Those who would take over the Earth and manage it I see they cannot grasp it; for the Earth is a spiritual vessel and cannot be forced. Whoever grasps it loses it."

The intent and content of this book is to elaborate on a new vision, a myth based in part upon those deep instinctual memories of a past Golden Age when the First People lived in harmony with the Earth: and also based in part upon the inherent flaws of the technocratic and materialistic world view of global industrial imperialism. These are fast becoming the Promethean nemesis of our civilization. We must find the humility and courage to acknowledge that the myth of an industrial utopia must be abandoned and replaced with a new vision to sustain us through this time of crisis; a new vision for transformation and renewal.

Are we fated to be destroyers of a world we cannot live without if we are to remain human? Loren Eiseley in the *Invisible Pyramid* suggested, "Perhaps, *Homo sapiens*, the wise, is himself only a mechanism in a parasitic cycle, an instrument for the transferrence, ultimately, of a more invulnerable and heartless version of himself. Or again, the dark may bring him wisdom." ■

CHAPTER I

THE NEW EDEN

There is an archetypal memory in all contemporary cultures of a past Golden Age. It was a time of peace and plenty. From this racial memory arises the mythic garden of Eden, our original home: the place where the First People lived.

The dawn of modern man came with the Eve of Adam—the last of the First People that we can remember once we feel into the deep marrow of our longing; our longing for the garden paradise of our species' childhood.

Mythologist Joseph Campbell observes: "When man ate the fruit of the first tree, the tree of knowledge of good and evil, he was expelled from the Garden. The Garden is the place of unity, of non-duality of male and female, good and evil, God and human beings. You eat the duality and you are on the way out. The tree of coming back to the Garden is the tree of immortal life, where you know that I and the father are one."

Loren Eisley put it this way: "The Eden of the eternal present that the animal world had known for ages was shattered at last. Through the human mind, time and darkness, good and evil would enter and poison the world."

After Adam and Eve man began to change the world rather than live with the world. Wild animals were domesticated, along with a small variety of plants. Before Adam and Eve, we were gatherers and hunters. The carnivore in man was tender for sacred were the prey. The First People were wise, taking no more from life than what would satisfy their most basic, simple needs. This was their law.

This law they learned from their mother-teacher—Nature. They saw the law around them, as a Blue Jay swooping down to seize a grasshopper, to feed her young. (There were probably no crazed grasshoppers turned into locusts then. They came as changed, frenzied, and ravenous beings soon after man began to change the land). They saw how life gave to other life and how other life took only as much as it needed. Life sustained life in the embrace of mutual interdependence, where cooperation and competition were subtly balanced. The insects sustained their lives from the plants and stimulated the plants to vigorous proliferation. And those carnivores who ate living creatures gave to them and to the earth by regulating their numbers and so helped preserve the health and vitality of herbivorous animals.

The First People were omnivorous; as hunters they were respectful of their prey knowing that if they ever killed more than they needed to feed themselves, the game would soon disappear. And as gatherers, they took freely what they might carry and store from the seeds, fruits, tubers, and leaves of myriad plants. They had great wisdom in both hunting and foraging. In many regions the First People migrated with the seasons and with the rains along with many other migratory species. Time was cyclical, and their lives were in rhythm with Earth.

Over millenia, we changed with the Earth, becoming its most self-conscious element. And then we began to change the Earth. Our fall from grace or loss of innocence is linked with the axing and burning of the forests to encourage more game, which were domesticated and either followed along the old seasonal migration trails or were herded around agricultural settlements. These settlements expanded, cities and industries evolved, and the wildlands and "wild people" were taken over. Swamps were drained, rivers dammed, and man was damned to drain and exhaust the Earth and to convert the natural world into an industrialized empire. (America now has what is called Industrial Parks—acres of factories, offices, warehouses, and parking lots; and Wildlife Refuges, where hunting, trapping and fishing are not only sanctioned but encouraged; and now we even have Theme Parks where wild creatures in synthetic surroundings animate these shallow places of public entertainment.)

It is not possible to restore the original Eden. We cannot return to that primal state of innocence that the First People, our ancestral parents, enjoyed and celebrated. Paradise is lost. But it can be regained: a New Eden can be created. We have the skill to turn the sickly industrialized wasteland that much of humanity now occupies into a healthy and healthful, truly civilized environment.

But do we have the will? Not without the vision. To have vision we must have feeling—empathy and love for the whole of Creation. Through reverence for the Creator or out of purely utilitarian concern for the emotional and physical wellbeing of our children's children, we must begin to love all things—plants, rocks, soil, rivers, and all. To love them with the same passion and protectiveness as we do our spouses and children. To love them with the same respect and gratitude as our own parents, and with the same understanding and fellow-feeling as our own brothers and sisters, knowing that we are all one. To harm the Earth and those who have their being therein is to harm oneself.

This harm arises when we discount the being of others—the sanctity of their being—and come to treat others purely as a means to satisfy our own ends.

When we began to change the world and remake the Creation into our own image—this was the "fall" of humankind. The advent of agriculture, the first industry (as distinct from the First People's crafts of fire and flint-tool making, music, dance, healing, and art) was our first step toward the bioindustrialism of today. Our disruptive hydroelectric dam systems, toxic chemical agribusiness and forestry enterprises, nuclear reactors and weaponry, misapplied genetic engineering are tangible proof of a fall from grace.

It is worth reflecting upon the fact that many good thinkers link the fall of man with domestication of animals simply for consumption and profit. They point out that before God's covenant was broken, humans were vegetarians.* Then after the Flood, we were allowed to eat meat. Thus, they agree, it is prudent to consider the wisdom of vegetarianism, which is one major way toward creating a New Eden. Considering the vast number of people who now populate this planet of finite resources, it is obvious that we must become gentle herbivores or conscientious omnivores who eat less meat. But we have become *unconscious carnivores*, ignorant of the cruel conditions in which farm animals must be kept if farmers are to make a profit; and unaware of the fact that the more meat we produce and consume, the more land is needed to raise feed for the incarcerated and drugged factory-farmed animals we consume. The meat industry, like most other industries, including the medical research and "health" industry (which still justifies the vivisection of animals) is pushing wildlife toward extinction.

If the fall of humanity means in part the extinction of other species, then our redemption to some measure must entail the preservation of other species. This in turn entails the protection and restoration of their natural habitats—not their incarceration in zoos.

---

* In actuality our ancestors were gatherer-hunters.

Instead of being apathetic and helpless bystanders, participants in the holocaust of the animal kingdom and the industrialized desecration of Nature, we can begin by being conscientious consumers, taking only as much, if not less, from life as we can give back to life.

Giving to life, by consuming less, especially meat, and buying or bartering recycled clothes and furniture, should be seen not as ascetic "crusader" martyrdom, but as the gentle way toward the New Eden. Seeking alternative medical help (not based upon the iatrogenic medical paradigm that justifies the suffering of animals in laboratories) and assuming greater responsibility for one's health by disengaging from culturally-conditioned consumer habits, are also ways toward the New Eden. And supporting those farmers who practice organic agriculture that helps regenerate the soil and not contaminate it with pesticides and other harmful chemicals is another responsible choice.

For some, this way is enlightened self-interest. But for others, it means the end: the end of a way of life whose values and perceptions of the world are not consonant with the continuation of life on Earth or with a sound and sustainable economy. The new gentle way is consonant with principles of humane planetary stewardship while living in communion with the whole of Creation.

To have reverence for all of Creation is not idolatry. It is the only way to show our praise and to glorify the Creator, manifested as divine presence in all of Nature's Creation. To do otherwise is to deny this presence, indeed reality itself. To assume dominion over the Creator and Creation alike is the blind hubris of our "fall" and is our nemesis of "original sin." This is the biblical meaning of the apocalypse, the uncovering or tearing of the veil of illusion that we have fabricated and which leads us to believe and act as though we are somehow separate from, if not superior to, the rest of Creation. ■

□ POSTSCRIPT FOR CHAPTER I □

The myth of Adam's two sons, Cain and Abel, is intriguing from the perspective of earlier civilizations coming into conflict. Abel was a herdsman, probably nomadic and a killer of animals, some of whom he sacrificed to Yahweh, god of Israel. Cain was probably respresentative of the Canaanite sedentary agriculturalists, (whose "offerings" to Yahweh were scorned). The conflict between these two 'sons' represents the war between the invading tribe of Abel with their great herds of domesticated animals and the agricultural settlements of Canaan, the 'promised land' of the Israelites. As Joseph Campbell has emphasized, the eventual subjugation of the Canaanites entailed also the supplanting of their earth-mother Goddess by the patriarchal god of the early Israelites. ■

CHAPTER II

LIVING HUMANELY

Ethical Decisions And Responsible Actions

How can we make this world a better place for all creatures? Our task of humane planetary stewardship is indeed almost overwhelming. It can make us feel hopeless and helpless when we come to know the suffering and destruction in the world under humankind's often unjust dominion. And our rage against injustice can impair our effectiveness when we judge others as inhumane and yet fail to show them the courtesy of compassion.

It is overwhelming to face the magnitude of our collective destructiveness of Nature, and our cruel exploitation of other animals. That the whole of creation "groaneth in its travail until now" with its floods, droughts, famines and epidemics of disease and war is a reality. But it is not all Nature's doing as ecologists and environmentalists are discovering. Everything is interconnected for we are all part of the one life. When we harm Nature, we ultimately harm ourselves: and when we are not compassionate toward other animals, we harm ourselves by our lack of compassion toward each other, for compassion is boundless or it does not exist. When we destroy the forests and wildlife therein, we cause floods, droughts and famines. The Earth is our home and when we mistreat it, all who dwell therein are harmed. When we rationalize the subordination and suffering of animals for "the benefit of human society," we destroy the ethical principle that sustains all societies: compassion. If we do not live by the *true Golden Rule*—do unto other life forms, as we would have them do unto us—human society suffers. Compassion is total, embracing all living things, otherwise it is a masquerade of sentimentality and patronage.

We should strive, step by step, to live by the Golden Rule, even at the risk of alienating those who see us as too idealistic or obsessed. When a thousand people make one simple and fundamental change in their life-styles, like bicycling to work, not wearing furs, or eating less meat, they reduce the rate of entropy; of energy consumption, pollution, and animal suffering.

The unnatural, man-caused suffering of the animal

kingdom is a symptom of the wrongness of our relationship with the rest of life. The extinction of species is a consequence. We may feel hopeless about all of this, or powerless, but we need feel neither. We each have the power to assume greater responsibility for our lives so that the way we live does not harm other living things.

We have the power of compassion, what Mahatma Gandhi called *satyagraha*, the power of truth in action. It entails loving thine enemy as thyself. If we would have others treat animals with love and respect, and have reverence for all life, then we must extend respect, if not compassion and humility, toward them. Otherwise they will feel misjudged and not understand our concern. Farmers who run cruel animal factories are not all cruel and ignorant people; they have been coerced into doing so by the competitive economic treadmill of agribusiness which we should all work to change. Biomedical and other scientists who vivisect animals are not all deliberately cruel persons. Their motives are generally altruistic, if not overly human-centered. We need their collaboration to instigate alternatives and new paradigms that will reduce and some day eliminate the need to make animals suffer in the name of science and progress.

This is not to imply that people never treat animals indifferently and even cruelly, or each other. Ethical blindness, erroneous beliefs (animals don't have emotions) and a host of rationalizations (economic necessity and medical progress) help those who exploit animals to ease their consciences. When empathy—the bridge of compassion—is cut, others' suffering is objectified and is no longer felt. But it is still there and it cannot be denied. The humanitarian can appeal to reason and objectively prove that animals suffer, but the greatest challenge is to help others open their hearts and feel the animals' suffering. People don't want to suffer in this way, but it is the only way to awaken compassion.

Dealing with institutionalized forms of inhumane animal exploitation takes teamwork and specialist expertise, as witness the legislators, scientists, attorneys, investigators, educators, fund raisers, and support staff who are employed by humane and conservation organizations. Likewise teamwork and specialist expertise is needed in dealing with global issues such as deforestation, the extinction of endangered species and acid rain. Without the support of a concerned and informed public, progress would indeed be limited. "Put your money where your heart is," is a relevant cliché, which people can do to help make this world a better place for humankind and animalkind alike.

The other cliché, to think globally and act locally, entails more than sending money to one's favorite cause or charity. This involves self-scrutiny and assessing how one's life-style and consumer habits may contribute, directly or indirectly, to animal suffering and to the pollution and destruction of the environment. To be a conscientious consumer is to assert one's power as an individual: to be the kind of person who can think globally and act responsibly. It is through these small acts of commitment to the humane ethic that significant progress can be made. Consumer citizens have great power which they can wield to make this world a better place for all. There is our hope. Most people do care, once they are informed, have viable choices and do not feel judged by humane crusaders for being insensitive and ignorant. Indeed such judgments are in themselves insensitive and ignorant of the inherent goodness in the hearts of most people.

In addition to supporting national organizations that are dealing with the more global and institutionalized aspects of animal suffering, extinction and the destruction of Nature, Humanitarians can become conscientious consumers at the local level to help make this world a better place. Conscientious consumers are mindful of the following concerns and can help steer society toward a more responsible and humane way of life and in the process, support those industries and entrepreneurs whose products and services are more ethical—humane and ecologically sound.

1. Find and support your local baker or food co-op. Agribusiness processed food products are laced with non-essential preservatives and other chemicals which have been safety-tested on laboratory animals. Many of these are widely used even though animal tests indicate they are hazardous to our health. These chemicals, like fungicides in bread, are deemed essential to prevent spoilage. But they are a product of a monopolistic over-centralization of food distribution. Likewise agribusiness uses pesticides and other agripoisons, antibiotics and other drugs on farm animals that are hazardous to wildlife, the environment and consumers alike. It is claimed that this is the only way to produce food efficiently and thus at lowest cost to consumers. The alternatives are to cook "from scratch" and to select organically-raised produce primarily of vegetable origin from local farmers' markets, food co-ops and health stores.

2. It is a wise decision to avoid eating imported fruits and vegetables out of season. These crops from other countries rarely provide any cash returns to the native peoples, many of whom are disenfranchised and formerly subsistence peasant farmers. Also the wholesale and unregulated use of agrichemicals contaminate these

foods, as pesticides and other agripoisons banned for use in the U.S. are exported and eventually come back to our tables in these imports. Furthermore, the destruction of tropical rain forests in South and Central America for the U.S. beef and fast-food hamburger markets and the destruction of sustainable peasant farms to make way for corporate pineapple, banana, coffee, and soybean plantations are well documented atrocities.

3. As conscientious consumers, humanitarians can set the trend of eating no meat that has been inhumanely raised, transported, and slaughtered, or even no farm animal products if they feel livestock treatment cannot be fully humane, or that the production of meat is a waste of nonrenewable resources.

4. Around the home and garden, we can all avoid the use of pesticides, detergents and other chemicals that have been tested pointlessly on laboratory animals and which are a hazard to one's family, animal companions, and wildlife that enter one's property.

Wildlife and a host of beneficial insects can be encouraged to come into one's garden by planting wild flowers, grasses, trees and shrubs. Large lawns and formal gardens require regular watering, mowing, and weed killer applications. A wild garden needs no pesticides nor weed killers, and conserves resources since regular watering and mowing is unnecessary.

5. In the house, the humane homemaker can set the trend to conserve resources and energy by properly insulating the house and restoring an old house rather than building a new one. Resource conservation even includes buying and refinishing old furniture rather than purchasing new furniture, especially that made from exotic imported woods from rapidly disappearing tropical forests. Recycle all possible materials from old clothes and newspapers, bottles, jars, cans and even food (which can be turned into garden compost).

6. Likewise, conscientious consumers purchase clothing from natural materials which are healthier to wear than synthetics which are wasteful of fossil fuels in their manufacture. While some concerned consumers even buy recycled clothing, all certainly avoid wearing the furs of live-trapped and ranch-raised animals; and question the wearing of wool products because of inhumane methods of sheep husbandry and predator control.

7. Organized medicine has opposed many nontraditional medical practices, such as homeopathy, herbal medicine, chiropracty, nutritional therapy, and until recently even counseling, acupuncture and meditation.

All these therapeutic approaches, which have not entailed animal research and testing, are valid alternatives to modern allopathic medicine and are part of the new holistic or mind-body medicine that many human and animal doctors are beginning to integrate into their practice.

To maintain a diet and life-style that is conducive to one's overall physical and psychological health and well-being helps reduce one's dependence upon the drugs, surgery, and other costly and often harmful ministrations of the medical-industrial complex, most of which were devised and developed on laboratory animals.

8. Avoid cosmetics that contain ingredients of animal origin and that have been safety-tested on laboratory animals. Conscience dictates that we buy old brands of various products, not new and improved ones that have probably been tested on animals first.

9. Another aspect of living conscientiously is investing with conscience. Individuals and organizations who invest in corporations that do the opposite of what their investors believe in, such as manufacturing pesticides, polluting the environment, and subjecting laboratory animals to scientifically dubious and often invalid toxicity and other tests, place themselves in an ethically com-

promising and contradictory position. Sometimes, but rarely, can shareholders prevail in bringing about reforms in corporate policy and ethics.

10. Every action, from flushing the toilet to using disposable plates and not discarding anything that might be recycled, entails an ethical choice. To act with conscience necessitates both knowledge and sensitivity. Parents and educators alike need to inform and sensitize children to adopt appropriate values and life-styles which do not violate others' rights or support those industries and institutions that are ethically unsound in terms of environmental impact, public good, and the well-being of animals. Responsible, humane planetary citizenship and stewardship may then be more than some impossible dream. ■

☐ STEPS TOWARD THE NEW EDEN ☐

We need a new measure for what we call our standard of living. This is not so much a function of the Gross National Product and of available goods, services, and jobs as it is determined by the quality of our relationships with each other, animals and the environment. As Mahatma Gandhi observed, the greatness of a nation and its moral progress can be determined by the way in which people treat animals. Animals, like people and Nature, are treated as resources by this and other technocratic nations that see economic determinism as the supreme ethic and the GNP as the definitive measure of the nation's well-being. But how can they be, when the quality of the environment is declining; when our relationship with the animal kingdom reflects a lack of respect and compassion, and when the basic rights of human and non-human beings alike are sacrificed to these materialistic ends?

The values of contemporary society are derived in part from the sanctified belief in man's unconditional dominion over the rest of God's creation; that only humans have rights and that animals and Nature were created primarily for our own exclusive use. This self-serving belief is reinforced by an attitude toward animals that denies them feelings, interests, rights and souls, or inherent divinity. With this world view, a state of mind prevails that cannot see or allow one to feel the inherent divinity in Nature and all living things, and to experience kinship with all life. It gives rise to a political attitude toward non-human life that we might best call biological fascism. It results in the violation of animals' rights and the destruction of the natural world.

Animal rights philosophy has taken the humane movement to the threshold of acknowledging the inherent divinity of animals, which puts the movement in a position that is anathema to the *status quo* and *modus operandi* of the technocratic civilization in which we presently abide.

If we are to survive as humane beings and not lose those attributes of the higher self that we know as humility, compassion and empathy toward all life, then we must now follow a different evolutionary path. Pure economic determinism and utilitarian materialism are self-limiting and ultimately self and world destroying. These values must become balanced by liberation spirituality of the "deep" ecology and animal protection movements, which are becoming an integral part of school and college curricula.

To paraphrase Albert Schweitzer and Sioux Medicine Man Black Elk, we may conclude that we shall never know world peace until we learn to live in harmony with the Power of the world as it lives and moves and does its work, and embrace all creatures in the same circle of compassion as we now embrace our own kith and kin.

The humane, ecologically conscientious citizen-consumer endeavors to live in harmony with this Power, with the laws of Nature and with respect for the rights of fellow earth citizens, human and non-human alike. Religiously, this is the path of pantheism or panentheism—respect for the inherent divinity in all of God's creatures and creation.

As John Hoyt, president of The Humane Society of the United States, has recently stated, the animal protection movement is to animals what the religious movement is to human beings. Both seek to imbue the individual with dignity and worth and to evoke caring for one toward the other, for the sake of the other. While John Hoyt has rightly called the movement a religion without a theology in the traditional sense, a new spiritual perception is emerging. Some call it ecosophy—the spiritual philosophy-theology of the "deep" ecology movement; others call it pantheism or panentheism—reverence for the inherent divinity in all of God's creation. This new spiritual perception of Earth and of creation recognizes the biological, ecological, and spiritual kinship between human and non-human life.

We *can* have a religion without a theology as we can likewise have an ethics without philosophy.* The supreme ethic of love as respect, compassion and reverence for all life is a matter of perception, of how we see the world and relate to other living beings. The very existence of other beings, miraculous and mysterious as it is, is surely evidence enough that they are worthy of our moral concern and respect for their inherent nature or beingness.

---

*For example, see James C. Edwards, *Ethics Without Philosophy: Wittgenstein and the Moral Life,* Gainesville, University of Florida 1982.

Sensing, feeling and acknowledging the inherent divinity in all things is the essence of panentheism. This is not a philosophy or a theology, so much as it is a condition of perception, awareness and relationship with other beings. The ethics and morality, what Buddhists call right heart, right mind, and right action, arise spontaneously from this condition.

Panentheism is thus not a theology, but a way of life. As the American Indian Rolling Thunder** declared, "understanding begins with love and respect. It begins with respect for the Great Spirit, and the Great Spirit is the life that is in all things—all creatures and plants and even the rocks and the minerals. All things—and I mean *all* things—have their own will and their own way and their own purpose; this is to be respected. Such respect is not a feeling or an attitude only. It's a way of life. Such respect means that we never stop realizing and never neglect to carry out our obligations to our selves and our environment."

The religious nature of the humane movement was expressed in the first annual report of The Humane Soci-

---

**Doug Boyd, *Rolling Thunder.* New York. Delta. 1974.

ety of the United States thirty years ago by Robert J. Chenoweth, Chairman of the Board. "Our creed is that love and compassion are due from the strong to the weak—I might say that man is to live by the Golden Rule, with the rule extending to the lowest of earth's creatures. If we hold this creed, then we are morally bound to be teachers and preachers and evangelists." Thus, the religious nature of the animal welfare-rights movement has been long recognized. What of the spirituality of the movement? Animal rights philosophy is the stepping-stone to this next level of concern and consideration and is not an end in itself.

If we accept that religion is a major determinant of morality, then it would be prudent to examine the role that religion plays in influencing peoples' treatment of animals and nature. The humane and "deep" ecology movements, along with animal rights philosophy, become transformed into a religion when there is devotion or reverence.

Panentheism as reverence for the sacredness of Earth and for the inherent divinity of animals and all living things is not pagan, animistic idolatry. It is a view shared by many religions: In Hindusm in the proclamation, "We bow to all beings with great reverence in the thought and knowledge that God enters into them through fractioning Himself as living creatures (*The Bhagavad Gita*) and in Christianity when St. Paul speaks of "one God who is Father of all, over all through all and within all" (*Ephesians* 4:6)

Philosopher Harold W. Wood Jr.* observes: "In conventional American religion, things like recycling, energy conservation, not wearing furs, even political action to preserve wilderness or wildlife, ordinarily have no relevance to religion. However, such behavioral modifications from a pantheist perspective can be justified as a religious undertaking. . . .The identification of sacredness in the earth demands reverent behavior. In turn, such behavior necessitates a personal commitment toward living in greater harmony with the biosphere."

The suffering of the world can draw us closer in kinship with all life. It is a great challenge to endeavor to live humanely—with conscience, so as to help minimize our impact upon wildlife and Nature, and curtail our support as consumers of inhumane animal industries (such as factory farming and fur trapping). Humanitarians can rise to this challenge, and by example help others practice what they preach.

---

*Modern pantheism as an approach to environmental ethics. *Envir. Ethics* 7:151-63. 1985.

The serious environmental impact of ecologically unsound technologies and industries can no longer be ignored. Governments and corporations cannot fail to realize that they are acting unethically if they violate the rights of people and animals to a whole and healthy environment. Private interest and the public good need to be wedded in a concerted cooperative effort of global conservation and humane planetary stewardship. In the long-term, corporate self-interest and enlightened self-interest are one and the same.

Political, social, economic and ecological concerns are all relevant to the work of the animal protection movement and to those seeking ways to live more humanely—with conscience. The more we can minimize our negative impact upon the environment and the animal kingdom as consumers, the more we, as humanitarians, will be able to help others practice what we preach: to live simply so that others may simply live.

The starvation of millions of people today, the wars between nations, extinction of species, cruel exploitation of animals, global greenhouse effect and the poisoning of the environment and of our own bodies, are all interconnected with the way in which we choose to live.

We have, I believe, a moment's grace to preserve what is

left of the Earth by discovering that which is sacred within ourselves as within all things. This supreme goal is surely an evolutionary and survival imperative as it is a spiritual one with revolutionary implications. To live compassionately and with conscience, in reverence of all life, is the spiritual transformation that the humane, animal rights and ecology movements are helping bring about. Making compassion an integral part of our lifestyle today is an auspicious beginning for the millenium to come: and for the New Eden. ■

CHAPTER III

THE FIRST PEOPLE

All living things are interwoven each with the other; the tie is sacred, and nothing, or next to nothing, is alien to ought else.

—Marcus Aurelius

I who was born to die shall live. That the world of animals and the world of men may come together. I shall live.

—Inuit legend.

The Eden of the eternal present that the animal world had known for ages was shattered at last. Through the human mind, time and darkness, good and evil, would enter and possess the world.

—Loren Eisley

Just now one of the great historical missions of the primal people of the world is not simply to sustain their own traditions, but to recall the entire "civilized" world back to a more authentic mode of being. Our only hope is in a renewal of those primordial experiences out of which the shaping of our more sublime human qualities could take place.

—Thomas Berry

Any idea, person, or object can be a Medicine Wheel, a mirror, for man. The tiniest flower can be such a mirror, a wolf, a story, a touch, a religion, or a mountain top.

—Hyemeyohost Storm

□ THE FIRST DAWN □

We have a history most ancient before any word was written or even spoken. "A time before the thought, I am", and long before Adam when the dread of death was upon us. There was no sense of place or time, only an all abiding presence secure in the absence of memory and of expectation and embraced by that power of being inherent in a body sentient but not yet born of mind as self. This was the "I" that had always been and was yet to become, moving easily within an endless water womb with no sense of separation between the outside and the inside. Breathing was feeding was growing was multiplying and never dying. There was no sense of self or other because the outside was the inside and the inside was the outside. Then something slowly began to condense; began to dis-

:ill, to instill a sensation of light, giving self-direction through the darkness that was within and around that which did not exist before there was consciousness of light. Light gave movement direction and intention toward or away and thus a reference for the emerging self. There was something out there now that was not within; there was light and sight and separation between the seen and the seer. Light preceded the birth of sight. Light directed the birth of sight as Earth directs the birth of mind as Self.

There were many dawns unnamed before the first dawn was known. There was no knowing with the first seeing until the coming of the dawn evoked anticipation as we all awakened from the darkness of a dreamless interior. There were eyes before there was an "I". And there were countless dawns before the "I" awakened and turning toward the light felt itself warming to the day. And there were countless dawns before the feeling became the thought of light and hoped-for dawn, and the pleasure of unfolding into warmth. There were countless other dawns before the inside became the outside and the outside became the inside once again as before. Then mind and light and self were one. This was the first dawn of enlightenment where the new mind felt the unity of all, the light of self in all and the sacred unity of all in light, connecting all to its boundless center in all things. And in the appearing and disappearing of all things the new mind became aware of the dream that was dreaming it. So it was with the first people when they awakened and held in reverence the light within and the light without. This was the first dawn for humankind. ■

The First People: A Vision

The first people knew
The One Mind in many
And the many in the One.

The bear was sacred,
Like the wolf and the deer
And all creatures of the Earth.

The first people knew
The One Soul in many
And the many in the One.

So they lived in harmony
In reverence of all.
It was the Golden Age.

Once people were shamans
Who could enter the forest
And let the forest enter them.

Once those who were shamans
Could become what they beheld
And return with wisdom.

Once people shared wisdom
Of the Earth Mother and creature-kin,
Knowing the world in many ways.

Once people knew themselves
As eagle, bear, wolf, whale
And saw the whole with shaman eyes.

Once people played with wolves
And lovers like leopards.
People were gods and gods were people.

Once people sang with wolves
And lovers like mourning doves.
Now the forests are gone.

Once people slept with wolves
And lovers like winter stars,
And the gods are gone.

Nearly gone, wolves
The people, the earth,
And the gods but one.
Once the people saw God
In all. Now they see
But one above, and not in all.

■

In the beginning was the Word
And the first words shared
Gave names to things
And in this naming
Came the knowing of the world.

Each word expressed part
Of the mind
In all things named.

In every word that was a name
There was divinity:
Stone, bone, soil and seed
Were holy things
Like water, fire and wind,
Aspects of the living whole
Whose spirit breathed in sacred places;
In valley, desert, mountain,
Forest, ocean, lake and river,
In all living things
Called, recalled, and known by name.
In the naming of things
The sanctity of being
In word and song and prayer.

The first people were like the animals;
They knew no shame, guilt, guile,
For they were innocent.
They were innocent because they were whole.
Being whole they lived their own truth.
Being truthful they were fulfilled.
Being fulfilled they were made whole.
Being whole they were holy.

Being holy they were wise.
Being wise they lived in peace
With each other.
The dread of man
Was not upon any beast of the earth,
Nor upon any bird of the air,
Or anything that crept upon the ground,
Or upon any of the fish of the sea,

For the first people took no moving thing
Unto themselves as food.
Every herb yielding seed
And every tree in which was fruit
To them was food.

And they were well in body and soul,
Enjoying peace
Until the Fall
And their alienation from the animals
Who, ever since, have feared them.

Animals were once revered
Not as gods but because
They were of God.
The first people had the power
Of empathy so they could tell
What animals were feeling
And could heal them as themselves.
With them the creatures
Could enjoy communion
Because there was no fear:
Only fellow feeling.
The animals were drawn to them
Because they had the power
Of compassion,
Of love that heals.

There was no submission
To make creatures compliant
And so to submit to human domination,
Helpless dependency,
Obedient subservience.
Some creatures still
Share with us kinship of communion.
Still suffer and enjoy with us,
Mourn the loss of companionship
Teach us that love
Is illimitable and unconditional.
When we recognize the God in them
Their love is the God in us.

There was a time when people
Conversed with animals.
The subtle sounds and gestures
Of courtship, kinship, joy,
Fear, alarm, anger, contentment,
Were known and shared.

The universal language
Of emotion expressed intention
Connecting heart of humankind
With all animal kind:
Here was compassion's bridge.
But now this bridge is almost gone.
Few people have the mind
Of communion with animalkind,
The heart to feel kindred suffering
Under man's inhumane dominion.

Once there was a time when
The death of an old buffalo,
wolf, lion, crow, eagle
Was known and felt as loss by the people.
Being part of the Earth Spirit,
The people saw all creatures
As fellow beings. Some they knew
Well because they lived together.

Others they knew
As the great ones of their kind—
Spirit animals who had power
And presence, if not prescience,
For they seemed like elders,
Leaders, shamans. Others
Were brothers, sisters,
Mothers and fathers.
So the people mourned
The death of animals.
Today
Those who mourn the death of animals
Experience a dying of themselves,
Feeling that the Earth Spirit
Will become extinct
And with this loss
So too the human spirit
Will be gone. What will remain
But people who do not mourn?

When children lived close to animals
Of the air, waters, and the land,
They acquired wisdom,
In the industry of ant and beaver,
Weaver bird and honey bee,
They saw themselves.
Heron's feathers, afloat, lured fish.
Squirrels, preparing for winter, put nuts away.
Ailing bears, eating healing herbs, grew well again.
Spiders, spinning silken snares, caught meals without moving.

As each creature embodied certain powers,
So the children discovered theirs
And took part in that creature's name
Who, most resembling them
Became ally, totem, teacher
Source of power and wisdom.
Creatures were benefactors,
Mirrors of the dream of divinity
And humanity alike.

The first people, all in youth
Were helped to cross the river
by loving wiser elders
Who knew the rite of passage
Was a kind of death
That enabled all to see
The world another way.
And with this double vision,
People were made whole,
Seeing self in other
And the fragile unity of all.

The flutes of Paradise are silent
Scattered like broken bones
Among the refuse of this age
That has no history, no sense
Of the sacred or the whole.
We have great power
Over Nature, so we keep
Animals captive in the zoo
And call it conservation.
There is no place for them,
Displaced by our own kind.

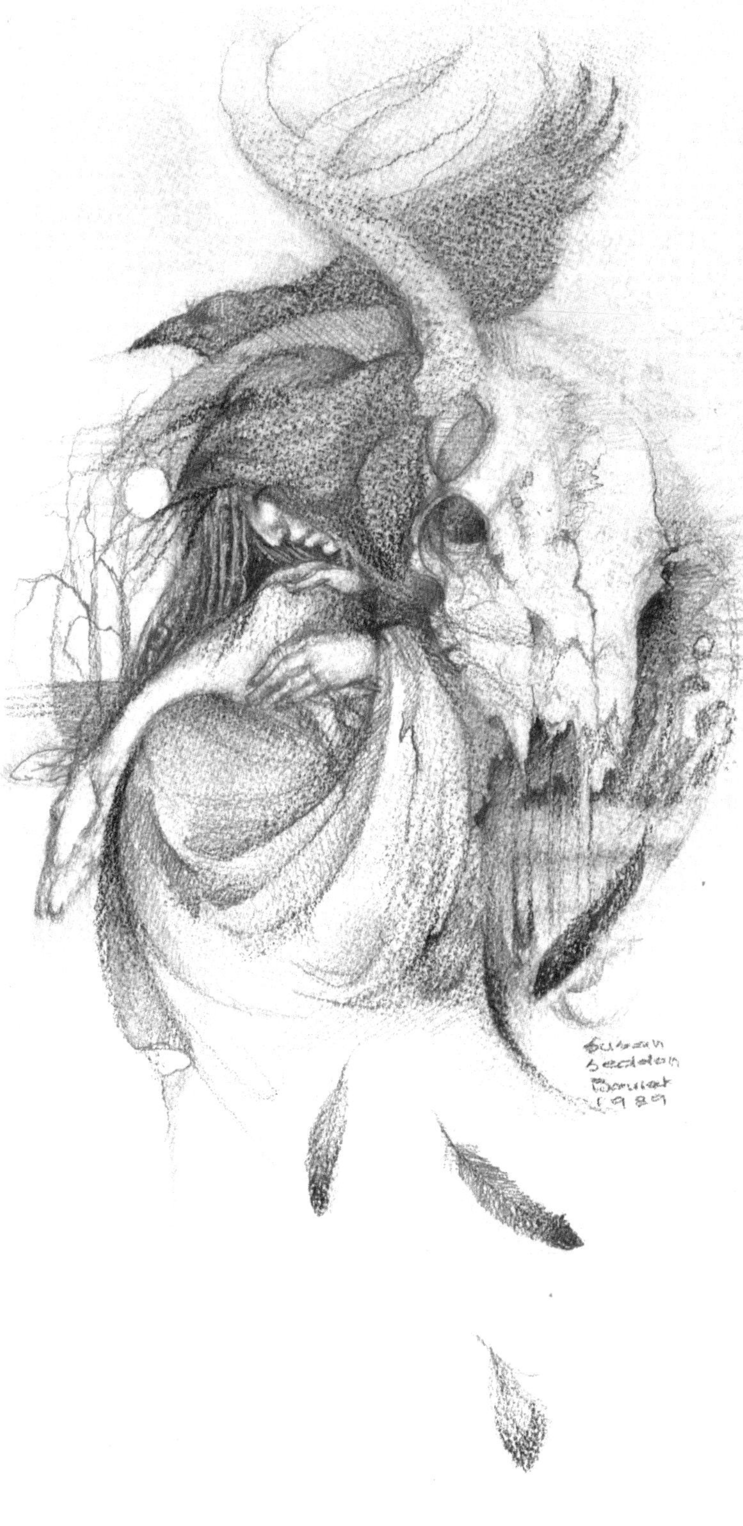
Susan
Seddon
Boulet
1989

What was Paradise
Is now deforested, poisoned land.
What point, when greed and need
Become synonymous? When ignorance
Is lack
And there is no why, no wonder
No way
Back to Paradise,
Until the flutes are found
And the bones make their music
Once again.

In your hand and mine
Is the hand of lizard and bear.
And in our eye is the eye
Of snake, hawk and wolf.
The blueprints of all beings
Overlap and share the imprint
Of God's seal—
The double helix of DNA.
We are of one creation,
Let not our diversity blind us
To our unity.

Where is the philosopher's stone,
The alchemist's gold
And the mystic's key?
In the cool of rock and shade of tree
As in the calls of mourning doves.
What is it in the rock,
The tree and mourning dove
That moves philosopher's stones
Makes gold from baser ores
And turns the mystic key?
That which is the touch of cool,
Enjoys the shade
And suffers the mourning doves
With joy and gratitude.
What gives omnipotence,
Transcendent power and grace?
All that we behold
In love and reverence:
All that we love illimitably
And without desire to keep,
To make over and over again
Forever into our own image
For we are not gods
Until we cease to strive
And know in whom abides
The rock, the tree and mourning dove.

Part dirt we are—humus and rock,
Part air and fire, water and manure.
Part of us stardust and sunlight.
Swamp mist, ocean fog, desert wind.
We are the forests and lakes,
Mountain ranges and prairie hills,
A part of all
As in our hearing, when our spirits soar
To the rising song of the meadowlark.
As in our seeing, when our spirits dive
To the deep world of the blue whale.
As in our touching when our spirits merge
With rock, feather, fur and skin.
As in our speaking, when our spirits know
The heart and mind of another.
When I am gone from this life
If you do not feel me in the wind,
The sun, darkness and light
The earth, water
—Even the food you taste—
The flowers you find,
Then you have never loved:
Never loved yourself
In these things,
And you have never known me.

If you feel me in them
As I am here, alive,
Then you know sun,
Darkness, light,
Earth, water and the food
You eat, the flowers you find,
The dirt, humus and rock
Of each of us, living and dead.

As we lose the feeling in our bones
Of oneness with the trees, the rivers
With the shrines of unhewn stone
And with all natural things,
We extinguish deep within us
The First People's spirit in us.
We will know that they are gone
When nature is no more.
What or whom then shall we be?
—Rulers of a vanquished Earth
Of some Industrial Empire
Void of spirit and of meaning—
Frenzied beings once quite human
Like the world
Once natural, whole and beautiful.

We have a moment's grace
To feel the Earth, now crucified
And suffer it to save it
So that we, the First People
Redeemed in spirit, shall be free.

When there was wisdom
And no selfish dreams:
When there was feeling
And reverence
For all natural things
We knew we were of dust and stars,
Of rivers, rocks and desert winds;
Of kestrel sky and deer wood musk.
"Maka Kin le Wakan—
This Earth is Sacred"
The old ones said,
And all our relations.
Mind, like love was then illimitable.
There was no fear of death,
Embraced as part of life
Along with all the suffering
It was accepted as the way
To compassion, wisdom and abiding peace.

Those who live in Sacred Places
Know how to live in a sacred way.
And if you feel and love
And dream and work in sacred ways
You may live in a Sacred Place.

If you wish to live in a Sacred Place
Then you must live in a sacred way,
And when you feel and love
And dream and work in sacred ways,
The Place will be yours forever.

If you do not know a Sacred Place
And wish to live in a sacred way,
Then attune your heart to feel and love
As you dream and work where the wildlings grow
And living gently, cherish all.

When you find in yourself the Sacred Place
To live in a sacred way,
Your heart will be one with the Mother of All
And with the spirits of every place
That live and dream and work with you.

When you have a Sacred Vision
You will know.

Only the heart can tell you
What reason cannot know.
When the Sacred Vision is given
But is not recognized
And sanctified,
Then reason makes the world profane
And demeans the Self it bears.

□ P O S T S C R I P T □

I am grateful for the encouragement of Gerry Hausman and to Lotus Press for publishing my first book of poetry. Susan Boulet's fine illustrations are what I would have done, had I her talent. The poetic images in this book come from some ancient memories that have become ever more numinous in spite of the dark shadow of my intimacy with the holocaust of the animal kingdom. I have written over 30 books, including textbooks and children's books, dealing with understanding and caring for animals, exposing the cruelties of various forms of animal exploitation and encouraging a respect and reverence for all creatures and creation. Such titles as *The Soul of the Wolf, Agricide, Understanding Your Dog,* and *Returning to Eden* will be familiar to many readers. Others know me through my syndicated newspaper column *Ask Your*

Animal Doctor and *McCall's* monthly *Pet Life* page. I now direct the Center for Respect of Life and Environment, a new affiliate of The Humane Society of the United States, and we have many projects, reports, and video programs that may interest readers. These range from genetic engineering biotechnology and humane sustainable agriculture to religious perspectives on our relationships and responsibilities toward animals and Nature. (For more information, I can be reached at 2100 L Street, NW, Washington, DC 20037.)

My deepest wish is that we should all realize our kinship with all life and live accordingly, developing appropriate technologies, industries, and a global economy that preserve and enhance the beauty, diversity, and vitality of the Earth's creation that is "ours" only in sacred trust.

Michael W. Fox